Fraser Island

Australia

PANOSCAPES®
Peter Lik

WILDERNESS PRESS

"My total dedication and
obsession with photography has
taken me on journeys into many
remarkable areas throughout
Australia. I captured this collection of
images using a specialist panoramic
camera. Because of the wider field of
view, this format enables me to
portray the true spirit of Australia
on film. Upon viewing these images
I am sure you will share with me
the tranquility and solitude
I experienced whilst capturing
the stunning beauty of this country."

PeterLikPublishing

PO Box 2529 Cairns Queensland 4870 Australia
Telephone: (07) 4053 9000 **Fax:** (07) 4032 1277
sales@peterlik.com.au **www.peterlik.com.au**

For all stock photography enquiries contact

PETERLIKIMAGELIBRARY

PO Box 2529 Cairns Queensland 4870 Australia
Telephone: (07) 4053 9000 **Fax:** (07) 4032 1277
art@peterlik.com.au **www.peterlikimages.com**

© **Peter Lik Publishing** 2001 BK05
Reprinted 1998, 1999, 2000, 2001

® **Panoscapes** is a registered trademark of
Peter Lik Publishing Pty Ltd

ISBN 0 958 70024 9

Front cover - Lake McKenzie
Back cover - Pandanus at twilight - 75 Mile Beach
Title page - Waddy Point

Special thanks to Boydy - Legend

FRASER ISLAND

*F*raser Island, situated off the southern Queensland coast, is renowned for its special environmental diversity and has been protected since 1992 as a World Heritage listing. It is unique as the largest sand island in the world and is over 120km in length and covers an area of 165,280 hectares. The visitor is able to enjoy a variety of landscapes, from magnificent stretches of beach to colourful cliffs and gorges, rainforest, freshwater lakes and creeks and spectacular sandblows. Plant and wildlife species (in particular birds and dingoes) are abundant.

Freshwater creeks such as Wanggoolba at Central Station and Eli Creek on the eastern side, are the most prominent of the many creeks on the island. The water in the lakes on the island is too pure to support much life. An exception is Lake Wabby, which supports several varieties of fish. Lake McKenzie, one of the largest of the lakes, can be viewed from four-wheel drive circuits and walking tracks.

Large stands of satinays, brush-box, piccabeen and kauri palms occur in the sub-tropical rainforests. In addition to tall forests there are scrublands, scribbly gums and wallum banksia.

The island features sandblows such as Knifeblade, caused by the action of sand shifting across the island. There are seventy-two different coloured sands, the best of which occur north of Happy Valley. Indian Head, one of several rocky headlands, is the major landmark of the island and is found at the northern end of Seventy Five Mile Beach. Further north is Middle Rocks' Champagne Pools, a popular swimming hole. Waddy Point provides fishing and views from the lookout.

Aerial view of sandblows at Cathedral Beach.

Sandy Cape, the northernmost tip of Fraser Island.

The Pacific Ocean constantly pounds the Maheno shipwreck.

The changing colours of Lake McKenzie.

Overleaf: The graduated turquoise colours of Lake McKenzie.

Aerial view of Lake McKenzie.

Tail fluke of the impressive Humpback whale.

A Humpback whale breaching.

$\mathcal{W}$hales are the largest and most popular mammals to visit Fraser Island. The giant Humpback whales, which may grow to over 15 metres, spend their winters in the tropics, then travel south for summer feeding in the Antarctic seas. This migration of thousands of kilometres is an annual ritual. The Humpback whale is the most vocal of all whales as they sing a highpitched song underwater. On a calm day, this unusual sound can easily be heard above the oceans surface. Commercial whaling from 1952 - 1962 reduced the entire population of 10,000 Humpbacks migrating on Australia's east coast to 200 whales. After 1962, they were declared a protected species and since then their population in the Barrier Reef waters has gradually increased to 600. There are two different subgroups of whales - Whalebone whales and Toothed whales. The Whalebone whales strain small plankton from the ocean, whilst the Toothed whales are active predators and swallow fish and squid whole.

Dolphins are one of the friendliest inhabitants of the Great Barrier Reef. The Bottlenose dolphins enjoy playing in schools and often ride the bow waves of boats. These beautiful mammals prefer the tepid waters of the reef and grow to about 2 metres. Dolphins are now a protected species.

Schooling fish encircle a lone dolphin.

Magnificent Orchid Beach, looking south to Waddy Point.

Overleaf: Waddy Point wilderness.

The fluorescent colours of the Great Barrier Reef.

A Fire Urchin displays its incandescent colours.

$\mathcal{T}$he Great Barrier Reef Marine Park, the largest in the world, is situated north of Fraser Island. The availability of qualifying dive courses throughout the islands and coastal areas make it an enviable location for diving. Scuba diving on the reef is relatively easy and once certified, you can explore the endless coral gardens, see thousands of species of fish, shipwrecks and underwater canyons. This experience is possibly one of the world's greatest wilderness adventures.

$\mathcal{S}$tarfish, brittle stars, sea cucumbers, sea urchins and feather stars are the five creatures which belong to the Echinoderm group found on the reefs off Fraser Island. This ancient group of animals has fossil ancestors over 500 million years old. The starfish are common inhabitants of the shallow waters of reef lagoons and are easily located with their bright colours. Their characteristic shape is a star, with five arms radiating from a central body which they use to creep along the ocean floor.

North of Fraser Island, Lady Musgrave Island houses the perfect lagoon.

Wathumba Creek estuary.

Indian Head stands like a monolith over the Pacific Ocean.

The days first rays illuminate the rippling sands of Indian Head.

Twilight at Seventy Five Mile Beach.

Aerial view of Champagne Pools, in the foreground, to Waddy Point.

The azure waters of Indian Head.

Delicate foxtail ferns nestle amongst twisted gum trees.

Strangler fig tree.

Coloured sands, Cathedral Beach.

A dingo leaves his tracks over a sand dune at Indian Head.

The changing moods of the sand dunes on Fraser Island.

Twilight scenes of Fraser Island.

$\mathcal{F}$raser Island is the largest sand island in the world stretching for 123km. The incredible sand dunes which constantly change with the winds of time, are one of the many features of the island. Larger sand blows are areas of sand which move over and suffocate existing vegetation, creating mini deserts.

Eurong Beach Resort.

Fraser Island Retreat.

Twilight glow over Kingfisher Bay Resort.

Previous page: Champagne Pools provide excellent swimming.

Early morning fisherman on Seventy Five Mile Beach.

Lake Wabby formed when a sandblow filled a freshwater creek.

Photographers footprints.

Lake McKenzie.

Cathedral Beach.

Eli Creek.

Sparkling waters of Wanggoolba Creek.

A lone Pandanus reaches towards twilight skies on Seventy Five Mile Beach.

Perfect barrels at Middle Rocks.

A typical road on Fraser Island.

Twilight over the glowing sands of Knifeblade Sandblow.

Dingoes are the icons of Fraser Island.

Full moon casts its glow over the rippled sands of Fraser Island.

Early morning reflections at Lake McKenzie.

Overleaf: Awesome skies cast their glow over Fraser Island.

Twilight tranquility at Lake Garawongerra.